On Love and Life

On Love and Life

nieve

*"Life is the reason we are here,
Love is the reason we stay."*

- R. Clift

ON LOVE AND LIFE
COPYRIGHT © 2021, 2022 BY NIEVE.
ALL RIGHTS RESERVED.
NO PART OF THIS BOOK MAY BE REPRODUCED IN ANY FORM
WITHOUT WRITTEN PERMISSION FROM THE AUTHOR.

DESIGN & LAYOUT BY R. CLIFT. R.CLIFTPOETRY.COM

SECOND EDITION, 2022.

ISBN: 978-1-9196541-1-9 (EBOOK), 978-1-9196541-2-6 (PAPERBACK)

NIEVE
@WORDSBYNIEVE
WWW.WORDSBYNIEVE.COM

to those that stayed

Contents

On Love   11

the rise   13
the fall   45
the wonder of it all   79

On Life   121

the light   123
the dark   155
the finding a spark   193

acknowledgements   237
about the author   239

A Word to the Reader

This book is designed to be read
the same way it was written:
wrapped up in bed,
in a bubbly bath,
at a summer's day picnic,
on a long train ride,
with a cup of tea,
a cosy blanket,
fairy lights,
candles
and lots of
chocolate,
alone,
with an open mind
and an open heart

- *Be gentle with me*

On Love

the rise

nieve

I don't know how to explain it.

When you hear
rain
begin to start,
then you look out
and suddenly,
it's pouring

I get the same rush with you

Commuter Boy

I see you every week,
we exchange looks
in reflections,
through the gaps of seats,
the pages of a book

I wear my best outfit
on days I know you'll get on,
maybe one day I'll ask your name
or I'll ask where you're from

I want to know what it is
that makes you smile on the phone,
maybe one day
I'll get off at your stop,
maybe one day
you'll take me home

I drown in dreams of you,
and when I wake,
everything seems

inadequate

on love and life

You are so vast,
like literature
or poetry

With so much history,
I want to study you,
get lost
in your pages

and read enough to love you
even though I know

I'll never read it all

nieve

I could write a whole book
on the story you gave me in that single look

Paint me a lullaby,
I'll sing you a river,
you bring the sunshine
and love I'll deliver

We'll dance in the sky,
I'll swim in your hands,
let's live a life
no one else understands

If you give me any more butterflies
I'm going to have to start naming them

on love and life

I promise,
if you cover yourself in sugar
I will lick off every single grain,
never will love
have tasted so sweet

Why do you watch me brush my teeth?
You ask

    - Because everything you do is *magic* to me

When

My stomach flips for you,
my heart flutters,
my mind strips for you,
my soul declutters,
my legs open for you,
my lips part,
yes that sound
is the beating of my heart,
oh to be near you,
hold you once again,
but baby don't come
until I say *when*

The Warmth of You

Cold are the sheets you left me in,
cold as the coffee you didn't finish,
cold as the colours that paint the broken sky
from outside

but here I lay forever warm,
holding your love inside me,
my body becomes a furnace,
burning on your memory

Look,

my

words,

they

are

falling

for you,

just
as
I
am

There Will Always Be Love

To know you,
is to watch the sun rise in the morning, thinking,
we have only just begun

to be with you,
is to hold a balloon, never wanting to let go

but to love you,
is to know that there will always be happiness

even though the balloon will pop
and the sun will set,
eventually

Distance

You are a whole ocean away,
but somehow,
are closer to me
than he who stands before me.
But isn't that how you know it's real?
When you're there,
when you're not there

My Honey

Your eyes are golden
like nectar,
your lips
so sweet and raw

Your hands,
I swear they're healing,
they're my craving
and my cure

When our bodies
intertwine,
all the bees,
they get in line

for never has a bee
created honey
quite like mine

I Know

I know you can't say the words
that I want you to,
not exactly,
your lips won't form the sentence

It makes no sense to me
that they are so afraid,
when your actions are so bold
and full of acceptance

but

when I feel you still watching me
even when I've looked away,
when you walk me to your door
but your eyes beg me to stay

you don't need to say it

When you pour me a drink
before you pour out your own,
when I hear the smile in your voice
as you say my name on the phone

you don't need to say it

When you grab me by the waist
and I completely let go,
you don't need to tell me then

I already know

nieve

I told him every thought I'd ever had
and he told me
I was the only thought
he could remember having

It was a split second,
but I knew I was yours

A Love Like This

Hold my hand,
never let go,
kiss my ear,
caress me so,
every second
with you is bliss,
oh I
have never known
a love
like this

Our Eden

There are no flowers
in our garden of Eden,
there are no apples
or trees,
the grass is not green
and the sky is not blue
and there aren't any animals
that roam with us too

and we don't have all
the time in the world,
and nothing is given for free,
but there is a place
where it's just me and you,
and that sounds like paradise to me

I could write a whole manual,
an exact how-to,
but still
no one could ever love me,
quite the way you do

You

You make an hour feel like ten minutes
and ten minutes like an hour,
you whisper such magic in my ear
it could turn a seed into a flower

I fit perfectly in your neck
like a bird in its nest,
you make summer the only season,
I don't care about the rest

If this is the sound of falling in love,
it's all I ever want to hear,
if this is the feeling of falling for you,
I never want it to disappear

Two people and nothing more,
that's all it's ever been,
they say that love is blind,
but I have never felt more seen

nieve

Your eyes are lighting,
they strike me so

When you tell me
you love my kindness,
I tell you
it's because I want to be kinder for you,
when you tell me
you admire my strength,
I tell you
I'm only strong so that you can lean on me,
when you tell me
you think I'm generous,
I tell you
it's because I give everything I have to you

I'm only me
because of you

- You make me a better person

I thought I knew what love was,
but you threw out every movie,
burnt all of the books,
re-wrote each fairy tale,
and now,
the dictionary turns to us

for a definition

The Music of This House

I fell in love with the music of this house,
the cracks and the creaks
and the heartbeat,
my favourite song
is the sound of you closing the door,
taking your shoes off,
coming home,
my favourite melody,
the sound of love being made
in the clinking of coffee cups,
the folding of bedsheets,
the lighting of fire,
and I could listen to it
all life long

Before We Met

Before we met
I already knew
what your voice sounded like,
your biggest turn on,
your wildest dream,
I already knew how to get you to come,
what words you would say.
Our love was not just predestined,
I'd already felt it
my whole life,
we did not just get drawn to each other
like magnets,
our bodies fused
like they were meant to,
why else would going out
feel so much like coming home

When the two of us met
we became one

How can you not have known
how much I loved you all this time?
I was sure the sunshine pouring out of me
would give me away

Falling in love with you
was like realising I could speak
a whole other language,
without ever being taught

the fall

nieve

Unexpected

The words,
they fall from your tongue
like snowflakes,
only to
invade my ears
like a swarm of bees

If Our Story Were a Movie

If our story were a movie,
upbeat music would play
as we danced across the square,
violins would sound
as we spent our first night together,
audiences would gasp
as you ran after me
and kissed me in the street,
and nobody would be prepared
for the final scene
when you left me

People are too used to happy endings

nieve

How can I go,
when I love even the bones of you

Default

When I can't sleep my mind runs to you,
default,
and I do everything to stop it.
But the memory,
it drags me in,
you always dragged me in.
And I'm living every kiss we ever shared,
every whisper,
every moment I ever thought
hey, look at me -
I'm finally living my movie.
Well, now it's stuck on repeat,
and it looks like
I'll never get to sleep

Bad Timing

You told me it was love,
a love that had to part,
it was just the wrong time,
not a change of heart

But that doesn't make it easier,
the understanding why,
the heart, it still breaks,
and tears, they still dry

Time, it seems,
shall be the reason and the cure,
I know deep down,
love doesn't wait to be sure

When You Left

It's been three days
and the earth doesn't seem the same,
the sun doesn't carry the same heat
in its rays,
strawberries no longer seem red,
just pink,
every night I close my eyes
but don't sleep a wink,
sunflowers don't seem to reach
the same height,
there is no longer sand,
only pebbles on the beach,
the stars don't shine as brightly
at night,
even a rainbow would be
black and white,
the sky
is no longer blue

I think when you left me,
the earth felt it too

Concrete

When did our love go
from concrete,
solid, tangible, together, real,
to concrete,
a mixture of broken things,
boring, common, convenient, cold,
a place
where cracks begin to show
and no flowers can grow

Empty Mornings

Our secrets lay spread
between hotel bed sheets
where we never lie,
empty mornings,
how love dusted the night,
sealed with a stamp kiss,
our voices only echoes,
the sound vacant tunnels miss

Material

Money bought us
many things,
a house,
a car,
golden rings

but money
can't buy
all things
that lack,

I never bought your love
with money
and money
can't buy it
back

Does She Love You

Does she fall asleep with her cheeks
on nothing but the mattress,
and do you tell her she looks beautiful

Does she sing to you or
read to you,
do things I didn't do

Does she tell you her secrets,
are they better than ones I told,
am I one of yours,
or has your memory grown cold

Does she sound the same as me
when she tells you *that feels good,*
has time found you a better lover
and a better love than I could

Does her laugh make you laugh,
do you laugh until you cry,
does
she love you as much as I did,
can
she love you like I

I whispered memories
in your ear
but all you heard
was a broken record

Before Me

How many before me
did you take to the beach
and walk to your favourite spot,
how many before me,
did you tell that you were afraid of love,
how many before me,
did you lie with in bed
until you are at least twenty minutes late
for work

I think of all these women
and wonder how many of them
loved you the same,
how many others
might be crying
over you too

How many of them
you hurt along the way,
and should I dare ask
how many more there will be,
and how many it will take
for you to change
    - or will you never change

and God knows how many more
it will take
for you to settle down.
I thought it could be me,
but that's what they all think

You were too much of a destructive force
for a woman like me

nieve

We were friends
before we were lovers
which makes it all the more painful
that now
we feel like strangers

Water is Water

Some days I don't think of you at all,
I just get on with my life.
But some days,
you're the only thing I think of,
and I can't do anything.
I thought heartbreak
would be a tsunami.
One devastating hit,
but slowly,
you recover,
re-build.
No one told me it was a wave,
constantly coming and going,
leaving me dry,
then soaking me through.
I guess water is just water
whatever its form

and I don't know how to get over that

Wilting

No matter what I do,
how much sunlight I breathe,
how tall I have grown,
you touch me
and I wilt,
you look at me,
and I wither,
back into the ground,
as if to worship the steps your feet have taken,
and I start picking petals off,
does he love me,
love me not

Where Does The Love Go?

When you leave someone,
but not because you stopped loving them,
where does the love go?

Does it ever go?
Does it take a different shape,
until it finds a different home
in a new heart?

Does it fade with time
like an old photograph?

Is it only ever temporarily lost,
until it resurfaces
when you hear that song,
go to that place

And if do you find it again
does it feel the same?

Where does the love go
when two people still feel it,
though they no longer feel each other?

Where does the love go
when one love
is replaced by a new love for another?

How can love just fade
as if it was never worth the fall,
and if it does truly leave,
was it ever love at all?

A Time

You're still here,
in every shower song I sing,
every time I close my eyes
and every drunken dream I'm in,
reminding me
that you are no longer mine,
but that you were,
if for a time

There are literally
seven billion
other people
on this planet
why
am I
so hung up
on you

Sponge

Just because I absorbed you,
soaked in all the love you gave,
does not mean I am your sponge.
You do not have permission
to wring me out,
leave me to dry

Slowly

Slowly
I shall forget
the taste of your mouth,
the curve of your back,
the tone of your voice.
I shall always remember your voice,
but it will never be yours,
only a prescription
of the past.
Right now you are a missing limb,
but slowly,
the more that time consumes you,
the more you shall become
light,
less of this dark,
this hole,
this missing piece.
Slowly,
you shall become just another day
I'm no longer living.
I will open the album,
and I will remember.
But the salt of the sea,
the wind-swept hair,
will be imagined,
a sweet sweet version
of history

If only it didn't have to happen
so slowly

Breadcrumbs

You leave me snippets
wherever you go,
they fall out of your pocket like breadcrumbs

As I gather them all
my tongue remembers
the familiar flavours,
but soon is hungry for more

I'm led to a house
that could be the place,
but no one lives here anymore.
The walls have grown sticky
and yellow

I turn around
to go back home,
back to myself this time,
but the crumbs have disintegrated
in my fingers

and I am truly lost

I'll have to remember
that childhood sweets
never taste quite
like you remember

and most of the time,
they are just bad for you anyway

Searching

Wondering where you went,
I tossed and turned in bed all night,
from anger to disappointment,
my lonely first night spent

Dangerous you were to me,
though dangerous you didn't feel,
but hiding in darkness all your life,
will never let you see

Into the light I finally came,
footprints nowhere to be found,
though harsh at first, the morning broke,
and finally let me forget your name

Let's Keep in Touch

You tell me
you still want to keep in touch,
oh don't worry,
I say,
we'll keep in touch,
through all the women you'll see
in the street
that look like me,
through all the pictures I'll post
of me living my life
without you,
in all of your lovers' arms
whilst you imagine
they are mine.
Don't worry,
I'm not going anywhere
just yet

The Greatest Loss

You might not feel it at first.
You might even forget about me
for a little while
as you start to suck the nectar
from other flowers.
But soon you will feel
the emptiness,
the craving that you can't seem to satisfy.
That's when the messaging will start,
the pining.
Everything you do will begin to feel
eighty percent,
mediocre.
You will start to have flashbacks
as you walk past places we used to go together,
and when you lay in bed at night,
the pillow next to you
will feel so empty,
even if it is not.
When I am gone you will realise
just how much you had,
and how much you didn't appreciate it.
Eventually you will settle down
with a woman who has little self-worth.
You will have fun together,
but you will still look at your grandchildren
and wonder what they would look like
with brown eyes
instead of blue.
You might not know it now,
but I will be the greatest loss
you ever knew

Velvet Love

You were smooth
and I was in need of smooth,
but smooth like silk.
Silk stills sleeping sighs,
the kind of thing you pay more for
but don't know why.
I tried,
but I can never sleep on silk,
it shimmers too much

I love like velvet,
crying out to be touched,
but you who aren't so rough as me
had had enough,
the softness in me was not quite right,
velvet smooth was not your appetite

I Put Our Love in a Box

It became easier when I realised
that loving
and loving you
are two separate things

So I put our love in a box
where it can remain intact,
lost in time,
the only place it can ever be,
in fact,
protected
from memory,
from sadness,
from history
repeating itself
        and I am stronger for it

It makes my heart hurt to think of us,
not because I miss you,
but because I miss feeling something

Maker

I wanted to apologise
for moulding you like clay,
giving you the words
I thought would make you stay,
and they did for a bit.
But while I thought I had
the world in my hand,
I was clutching onto sand,
and you sat counting the grains
as they slipped through my fingers,
and now fragment memory lingers

I tried to dress you up
because you walked barefoot
and I couldn't stand
how you'd drag through other's soot.
I gave you leather,
and metal moulded you
into my view.
I was doing what I thought was best,
and at the time I couldn't see
that I would never be,
I should have known
you were made of softer materials

nieve

You were always happier
in my dreams

Closure

We sat as if it was our very first date,
as if flowers, not weeds,
were flourishing between this silence,
and I wondered what we might look like
from the outside

We probably looked normal

And then it rained
and then it poured,
and we sat on the side lines,
watching laughter and Christmas lights
run circles before our eyes,
and we went out,
and we got soaked,
and my makeup ran down amongst tears,
and you took pictures

I was in a state of happy sad,
of nostalgic mad

But that night,
is the closest my life has ever felt like a movie,
and I found comfort in thinking
that maybe our ending
is already written out for us,
that maybe we should let it play out

Even though it's not me anymore
I hope there's someone loving you

   - You were made to be adored

the wonder of it all

Together we had the rise and the fall,
at least we can say
we had it all

We Were Both a Little Young

We were both a little young
when I met you and you met me
and I moved in next door
but you'd still walk me home

We were both a little young
when I left to travel the world
and you waited patiently,
my world at home

and I said I love you
and you said it too,
and we were both a little young
but we acted like we knew

Thinking about it,
I didn't know a thing,
but now that I do,
at least I admit when I don't,
and I admit this too:
I still think about you

How we were both a little young
when we made big decisions,
like when to stay
and when to go

and when rain fell from my cloud
and turned a grey
you had never seen before,
you didn't know how
to make it go away,
without going away

but we were both a little young
when your body wrapped round mine,
and though we've both moved on,
I still wonder if you're fine

and wonder how much of it
you remember too,
as bad,
as good,
as silly,
or as true,
and how much it stung,
when we were both a little young

One and Only

I could see
the wandering of your eyes
and knew
I was not the only sugar
in your life

I could hear
the beating of your heart
and knew
it did not beat
just for me

but I could feel
the whole of your embrace
and knew
it was not fake

Though not uniquely mine,
in your arms
it was always love

Superficial

People always ask what I saw in you,
but darling, it was never a case of seeing.
You were a feeling,
you were my awakening,
in you I felt sunshine,
a sunshine
that warmed me through and through,
and people may say I could do better,
but you made me happy,
you made me feel,
and for a time, it was real,
and that can never be denied

Feelings, they may come and go,
but the way you made me feel in that moment
is a pleasure I shall always know

Jarana

Our love was primitive,
smoke puffs and shared bedrooms,
city lights,
stay with you,
bandana

Working through the night,
I'd try to stay awake,
you were my party,
I your honey,
jarana

Ghost

I can still hear your laugh,
it echoes down my spine,
and I still feel the weight
of our bodies intertwine

The impression of your fingers
plays on the back of my hand,
and the linger of your kiss
is like a footprint in the sand

I still see your crooked smile,
showing the teeth you always hid,
baby you left,
but your love never did

Time taker,
why do I even try,
heart breaker,
why do I give you time,
love maker,
now I remember why

The Miles Between Us

If you told me
to come see you,
I would leave
this second
without packing
a single thing,
I would walk
and swim
and climb
across the miles
and oceans
and mountains
that lie between us,
arrive at your door,
blistered
and dripping
and breathless,
with open arms,

but you won't,

and so I

never will

- And so these miles stay between us still

nieve

I'm drunk on the idea of you,
and you
are the only one
who can sober me up

Is it love?

Is it love
if you are always waiting
until the early hours of the morning
for them to come home?
Is it love
if you have to ask yourself
what you did wrong
at least twice a day?
Is it love
if you wish things
could go back to the way
they used to be?
Or perhaps
a better question would be,
regardless of the love,
is it still worth it?

Too often do we confuse
love and lust,
considering they only share one letter

Always

I go to work
and I get the job done
and I do it by myself
with no help from anyone

I write a million words,
I've a million things to say
and I think of them all
in my own unique way

and when I go home
and as I rest my head,
there's no one lying with me
in my double bed

No, I don't need someone
to hold my hand
and I don't need any praise,
yet I do everything alone

but thinking of you
always

Story

I have our whole story
recorded in my mind,
it lives there so easy
to go back, to rewind

I watch us as lovers,
fall, so unafraid,
I watch us roll around
in the space that we made

There are parts I don't like to see,
but I still let them play,
I watch how I still loved you
where others would want to stray

But you can't pick and choose,
you can't have it both ways,
like any story, ours comprised
of happy and sad days

Some parts not are not PG,
I like to watch those too,
which episode shall I watch today,
wishing it was true?

on love and life

Just like riding a bike
or learning to swim,
I will never forget how to love you

Compromise

My first love
was not hot,
not passionate.
It was safe
and affectionate,
reliable
and happy.
My second love
was steamy,
rip your clothes off,
messy,
bloody,
unreliable
and teary.
But isn't it funny
how I would rather be trodden all over,
broken down
a million times,
repaired in one kiss,
and feel that love again,
the hurtful,
reckless kind,
than to be secure?
I need to find the in-between,
but I don't understand -
I thought love shouldn't be
a compromise

Our Place

Your place was north,
my place was south,
when we met in the middle,
I'd melt in your mouth

Your colour was red,
mine was sky blue,
but we made colours
of a different hue

But as time went on,
more often than not,
I was there,
and you forgot

But even though
it's over now,
I know we'll meet again
somehow

Love doesn't die,
it just departs,
and that's the hardest part of letting go -
trying not to grasp it as it goes,
trying not to find it, once it's gone

Visited

You looked better when I saw you last,
you had sunshine on your face,
golden were those days behind you,
like freckles from the heat,
you left with just a trace

Not to say you're not the same,
the eyes give you away,
you cracked a smile,
I heard your laugh,
and blonde peaked through the grey

Funny after all this time,
we still fit, like a lock and key,
as if the earth and stars knew
that to bring you back to life,
they'd have to bring you back first, to me

I wouldn't let a friend treat me this way,
so why do I put up with you,
wrapping up love
as an excuse

The Ways I Loved You

I have loved you
the way the ocean waves
love the beach

Relentlessly,
naturally,

I have loved you
even when that love
seemed far out of reach

Hopelessly,
desperately,

I have loved you
whilst counting all the reasons
I should not

Guiltily,
regretfully,

I think it's time I loved myself
with the same devotion,
for all this time I forgot

Consistently,
indefinitely

nieve

From all the loves I have ever known,
yours is the furthest I ever had to walk
to get back to myself,
but I got there eventually,
I always do

Someone Else

So you've found someone else

I'd be lying if I said I didn't feel anything,
so here's what I feel:
sad,
jealous,
irrelevant,
ache

But darling it's all the same -
why did you switch cars
only to drive down the same lane,
and those words that come out your mouth,
they're not the truth,
if you love her, you loved me
so where's all the proof?

Now I have found someone else too.
Myself.
And here's what I feel:
whole,
happy,
peace,
steady

I'd like you to meet her
but I don't think you're ready

Comfortable

It was hard at first
to take my clothes off
in front of you
and not feel the cold,
but over time,
sparks flew,
fire burnt,
and my clothes,
they learnt
to fall

I used to think that you
were the reason
for it all,
that I
was getting more comfortable
with you,
that we
were fusing,
but when you left
I never grew cold again

I was not becoming
comfortable
with you

I was becoming
comfortable
with myself

You were just my first
lucky spectator

A Different View

It was different with you,
life,
it had more taste,
more flavour,
everything was sweeter,
more bitter,
less blurred.
You taught me a way of living
that I never knew,
throwing stones without looking,
singing with eyes open,
and every day I still think
that life could be true

(for me, but without you)

A Letter to my Future Lover

I hope you can accept
that you will always be my second love,
because I have to love myself first and foremost.
But also know
that in doing so,
my love for you will never be half-hearted.
I shall give my whole and complete love to you,
because I too, shall be whole

Am I in love?
Not if you have to ask

Have you ever been in love?
No
Then how do you know it exists?
I have eyes, my dear

You Are Love

We are taught
that love is everything
and we are disappointed,
feel empty,
when it doesn't come easy
       - for the longest time this is how I felt

But love is everything,
as it is *in* everything

And to know that,
is not knowing that you have it all,
but that you've had it all,
all along

While you have been listening out
for those three magical words,
hoping that they will heal you,
you've had the power to heal yourself
with a love that will always hear you

A song,
hidden in plain sight,
in the
'drive safe's
and the
'sleep well's,

and it's singing,

you are loved,
you are loved,
you are love

After my first breakup
my two best friends
came round my house
armed with movies
and chocolate mousse,
and it was then that I knew
I was going to be okay.
My teenage heart had had
its first taste of love
and I was finally starting
to live life
independently,
and though the boys would come and go
and I didn't know what career I would have,
if I stayed with these girls,
we would all
be okay

- Our first real love is our friendships

It Always Comes Back Down to Love

Love always leaves me hating you,
love always leaves me hating,
love always leaves me,
love always,
love

Ours

We found it between sheets,
in the silences between words,
in broad daylight and the dark

I don't know if it was love,
but it was ours,
let us hold on to that
at least

on love and life

We will never get married,
we won't ever celebrate
our fifty, or even five year
anniversary,
but when I am old
and grey
and looking for an adventure,
we will find each other
and become teenagers again

Love still exists
in every corner of the earth
we have ever been together,
in every
thing
we ever touched,
it thrives
even when we
do not

Preparations

I spend every day looking for you,
thinking,
I'll know you when I see you,
thinking,
this could be it,
one day it will click,
but what if it's not a click,
what if it's a slow
connection,
how can you prepare for a love
when you don't know what form
it's going to take,
how can you give your heart away,
when you know
it could break

Growing Old Together

I long
to be able to hold hands
in silence,
knowing there is nothing
we need to say to each other,
because we've already said it all

I Have Always Known You

I have always known you,
our love for each other
is indescribable,
I leave you notes
in the shower steam,
pluck your eyebrows,
when you let me,
when I have trouble sleeping,
I listen to your heartbeat
and feel you breathing,
you say you wrote a song for me,
and you play it with your fingers
as they run down my spine,
I know all the words,
and you have always been mine,
baby,
I haven't met you yet,
but I know just who you are,
you've always been here
in my heart,
there has always been
a vacant room,
I'm waiting for you,
come home soon

Remember Me

I am no scientist,
no inventor.
I have not made
any groundbreaking discoveries.
I will not leave behind
a legacy,
I know.
But if I am not to go down in history
for the things that I have done,
then at least let me be remembered
by you,
for the way that I loved

On Life

the light

nieve

What might not look like much in winter
turns into a forest of flowers
come spring -
what kind of magic is that

Hometown

I am shaped by every brick in this town,
from the church bell to the market square
to the slide where I fell down,
from the market where I worked,
to the bandstand where I played,
the school where I made my friends
and the sweet shop that we'd raid.
But no matter how much I come to learn,
or how far my life
stays on track,
no matter where in the world I go,
I know I will always
find my way
back

Cambridge

Old, the city streets
stand still in time,
they always will.
Red brick and yellow stone,
colleges,
cathedrals,
I have always known
and never gone inside.
Pebbled pavements,
bicycles
and their people,
this city breathes more than I do

on love and life

Where there is life
there is beauty

Migration

If I could be a bird,
I would be a swallow,
to experience the miracle of migration

Who would not want to see
half the world
before their final destination

Miles of flying
and long, hard days,
many with starvation

But all worth it
to come home again
for the ultimate celebration

Ciutadella Park

Lovers walk hand in hand,
shaded by palm shadows and leaves,
at five o'clock the sun still shines
y todo el mundo es feliz.
It's easy to forget there is nature everywhere
when you live in a city and harden,
but then, what better place to live,
when you can have this as your garden

Lily of the Valley

Before I knew who you were,
you were gathering in woods,
green stems enclosed amongst
the whitest of hoods

Hanging down as if ashamed,
you knew you were not pure,
though white your petals are,
you hold poisonous allure

So much detail you possess,
that hold secrets, I can tell,
I found you one lonely day
and wished to know you well

I told you something private
in the hope you'd do the same,
and now the lilies of the valley
sing and call my name

I keep
picking
scratching
bruising
and all my body does
is keep
healing
healing
healing

The Mountain

The mountain does not ask to be conquered,
it does not ask for snow,
it does not know why the roads
are so windy,
it does not know where they go

It cannot help having high altitude
or confusing white with blue,
but what it does know, is that with
strong foundations
comes a magnificent view

Train People

Whenever I take the train
I am reminded of how easy it is
to let the mind slip away

I look around,
everyone is busy,
music,
phones,
laptops,
silent noise.
It's like they are afraid of their own thoughts

What is more beautiful
than the sky
when it cannot decide which colour to be,
so decides
to be them all

    - Sunsets

People walk in and out of your life
as easy as breathing.
You can decide who stays.
But when you've got a great friendship,
you'll know,
because it feels as easy as breathing

Sleep

If your days are filled
with work and ties,
lay down in bed
and close your eyes

If you need to dream
of a different time,
just go to sleep,
you'll be just fine

If you need to alter
your state of mind,
just close your eyes
and you will find

And if you're in pain,
just curl up tight
and go to sleep,
it will be alright

Balconies

Through each small window I get a glimpse
of the life you lead,
the life you shield

I see you in your dressing gown,
having a cigarette,
on the phone

Close enough to speak
to each other,
though we never do

Is this what city living is all about,
ignoring the lives closest to you,
people placed together by circumstance

I forget that this is a two way view
and wonder what you think of me,
looking back at you

nieve

You wanna know
how I know
that the sun and moon
are the best of friends,
even though they are so far apart?

They always step back to watch the other shine

There is Something More

I've seen it,
I've seen it in the sun,
over graves in the morning
when the day has just begun
and scattered beams light a thousand souls,
like death isn't something to be afraid of

I've felt it,
I've felt it through windows,
through closed glass
or open when the wind blows,
in stained glass patterns with ceilings so high,
but nothing seems out of reach

Suddenly it all made sense,
nothing so hazy
had ever been clearer,
and the theories,
they might sound crazy,
but they don't have to be certain

I don't know what or where or how,
but I know that I am sure,

there's a life to be lived,
and there is something more

Mona Lisa

I saw the Mona Lisa today,
she half smiled at the crowd
as they battled to see her,
she took up a whole wall,
though
she is actually quite small,
and on the other side of the room
hung a masterpiece,
to which no one cared at all

Spanish Rooftops

In Spain the houses look like blocks of stone,
but look at them from above
and you see a beautiful sea,
made with the colours of the sun

Human Honeycomb

Sitting in a café long enough for
the rain on your coat to dry,
talking of trivial things like war
and all of a sudden wondering why
the day is constantly dimming

And leaving a lipstick stain
on that mug from which you drank,
later, another soul cleans your claim,
goes home to his own tank
where he'll keep on swimming

The next day he's just over there
on the same path you roam,
unaware of that moment you share,
kept secret in the human honeycomb
that bound you in the beginning

Golden Hour

It's my favourite time of day.
The sunlight creeps in through the shutters,
cascades down the wall,
illuminates the whole hall

Even though it's cold outside
the brightness warms my skin

And where there is warmth,
there is hope.
Though the day is setting,
it isn't over yet

nieve

When the sun shines
so do I

on love and life

I am
the sum total
of every single person
I've ever met,
every place
I've ever been
and every day
I've ever breathed

Family

Even when you didn't know if I was coming home,
you always left the light on for me

Talking to The Moon

I've always loved the night
more than the day,
it's where my creativity breeds.
No matter how much I try to wake,
I never want to rise with the sun,
he steals all my thunder,
but the moon,
she lets me have the glory.
The moon knows that
I need illumination,
not blindness

The moon rotates round all of us,
but I can't help thinking
she's looking at me

nieve

It is of some comfort to me to know
that we are the same age,
that no matter where we are in the world,
how far apart,
we are still growing together

Three a.m.

There is something about
three a.m.,
the way it holds me still,
keeps me bound between its arms
in a way it always will

And in the morning when I wander
through the dirty city streets,
I think of how the traffic flows
with a million constant beats

How I would still rather lay in bed,
fighting sleep in the dark,
where inspiration would find me better
than strolling any park

Today I have done nothing at all
and I consider it
one of the most successful days of my life

Welcome to the World

Welcome to the world little darling,
take your first breath and dream,
open your eyes and see
what we have all been waiting for you to.
Hold this hand, this hand of mine,
remember to take your time to grow,
I hope you always know
how loved you are.
Baby you will go so far,
farther than the farthest star,
with all this love you have,
you have every power in the world

nieve

The most meaningful gift
I have ever been given
is time

the dark

nieve

Hate wraps around my body like ivy
and I water it everyday

When the boy who used to bully me
told me he was sorry,
the stars aligned as I forgave him,
but they come back every night
so I never forget

Unattainable

She smiles down at people,
looks seamless every day,
how happy, how beautiful she is,
what a life she has, they say.
She gets home, takes off her gown,
puts moisture on her face,
she goes to sleep, might even dream,
and wakes the next day
to do all the things you do,
and wish you did her way

Inner Battle

You do not place plants in a dark cupboard
and expect them to grow,
you do not throw a stone into the ocean
and expect it to float,
so why do you treat your body
like a dumping ground,
a boxing ring,
a bobbly jumper that needs
all the bobbles picked off,
and then expect it
to keep pumping blood,
breathing air,
as if everything is normal

These days I don't know
if the makeup I put on
is a mask,
or war paint

Candles

My father never let me light candles,
afraid that I would burn,
he has seen what loss looks like first hand

But I can never take anyone's word
for anything,
I have to feel things for myself

I like to watch the flicker,
sometimes I even put my finger in the flame

Now I light candles every day,
I guess I'll never learn

nieve

Every month I am reminded
just how much it hurts
to be a woman

If life is not a race
then why do I care so much
that you are always
ahead of me

Lonely

I am not alone,
there are people in my life,
but people come and go,
and now I'm the one who's gone

I've never been afraid of my own company,
but now that it's just me,
I'm starting to feel for the first time
what it's really like
to feel lonely

I don't know how we grew up together,
but at the same time,
grew apart

nieve

My father says
I am the best thing
that ever happened to him,
but I can't help wondering
what adventures,
what life
he might have had
without me

The Life of a Flower

The flowers bloom,
white, pink, green,
the focus of the room

Congratulations,
I'm sorry,
thank you,
I love you

The heads begin to sigh,
yellow, brown, black,
the flowers die

They were beautiful once,
but we do not grieve

We discard,
we replace,
we forget

but to the flower,
this was the one chance to be,
to see
a glimpse of human life
from a vase

As I throw the flowers away,
I wonder,
was the bloom worthwhile?
One life cut short,
to make another's day

The people look at me
with such surprise,
as if I had done something
miraculous,
in-explicable

   - All I did was smile

How much pressure
is put
on the shoulders
of sixteen,
how is anyone
supposed to know
who
they want to be

The world is your oyster,
what a daunting thing to hear

My Generation

Over qualified
and under-experienced,
that is what we are

We are told that life
is full of options now,
but that still doesn't get us far

And most of us,
to pay the bills,
go back to a café or bar

But I'll still fill out applications
though the future is unclear,
my confidence won't mar

And I'll still work hard
but also think it does no harm
to wish upon a star

nieve

I don't fear growing old,
I fear never getting the opportunity

Sick

I am sick of calling up
at eight on the dot,
every day
for a week on the trot,
just trying to get through
to a receptionist

I need to see a doctor,
a nurse or a physician,
or just anyone at all, that could listen

I am sick of joining
three month waiting lines
only to be asked
if I am pregnant
and being reminded
that everyone feels bad, sometimes

And I am sick of finally being seen
by another human being,
only to come out feeling
like Google
was actually more healing

If I was not sick before,
then I am now

nieve

The more I turn on the news
the less I recognise this Earth
as home

Tsunami

The water does not care
about the things in its way,
how long they took to build,
whether they deserve to stay

The water does not think at all
as it comes crashing down,
destroying everything before it,
a whole street, a whole town

The water does not know
how much time it will take,
to clean up the work of an hour,
how many eyes will not wake

While we see families and lives
ending in minutes, not years,
the ocean does not notice
the mingling of salt water and tears

And even with waves so high
that seemed like they would never stop,
the ocean does not feel the loss
of a single
drop

How tragic it is
that more often than not,
it takes a tragedy to bring people together

Change

It does not happen overnight,
but eventually it all adds up.
Those houses filled between mine
and my neighbours garden,
they all look the same.
We complain of the sun,
we complain of the rain,
we don't know whether to celebrate
or criticise the record heat,
but either way we cannot bear it.
I did not think about it
until I had to,
I don't think any of us did.
We do not worry about our teeth
until our gums bleed,
we do not care about our bones
until they break,
wake up,
pretty girl,
the earth is changing
and nothing is set in stone,
and if you don't do something about it,
who will?

nieve

How can we breathe,
when the lungs of the earth are on fire

Slow Revolution

When I passed my driving test
my father always said,
I don't worry about your skill,
I know that you can do it,
it's everyone else
that scares me.
How can you react, when a maniac
comes speeding around the bend?
And it's true.
You can't control
what other people do.
No matter how much progress
I make,
it does not matter,
if one person
recycles everything perfectly,
uses zero plastic,
grows all their own vegetables,
when the whole world is out driving chaos

How do we begin to repair such a mistake,
of not enough give
and too much take

Cancer

You never think it will happen to you,
it doesn't exist until it happens to you,
it's the one swear word
that everyone is afraid to say.
But now this word is a part of my life,
common as the light of day

nieve

What can a daughter do
when she sees her daddy cry,
when he has been the one to hold her hand,
keep her strong,
her whole life

Grandma

I don't know if I will ever forgive myself
for not coming to see you that weekend,
but how was I to know
it would be our last

Helpless

When your blood
decided to block the flow
of oxygen to your brain,
I could not help you then

When your eyes
decided to take a break,
and you slept for a very long time,
I could not help you then

When your mouth
decided to slump
into a half smile, half frown,
I could not help you then

And I could not help you now,
even if I wanted to.
I can talk to you,
hold your hand,
feed you and
give you hope -
I can do that
even when there is none left in me

But if I could not help you then,
then I cannot help you now

and now I don't know what to do

on love and life

It Used to Be You

It used to be you
who would comb my hair
and tell me it's going to be okay,
rub cream on my scars,
bandage my wounds
and promise me you would stay

Now I do it for you,
except I can't tell myself it'll be okay.
It makes me wonder
if you ever knew.
Was it always an empty promise?
I bring you food,
make your bed,
change your clothes

It breaks my heart
but what can I say,
it's the least I can do,
for the life you have given me

I have watched my father
look after his father,
and I see the strength in his arms.
What am I going to do
when the time comes
to do the same for him?
I do not have that strength
in my arms,
mind,
anywhere really

Balance

When it's good, it's good,
and rain feels like honey dripping on my skin.
When it's bad, it's bad,
and every dark cloud soaks me from within.
Teach me how to be balanced,
for it is something I have never known,
teach me how to live a life one side of the line,
I am sick of being 'fine'
instead of fine

Lullaby Lies

When you hold me tonight,
just tell me it's alright,
whisper sweetness in my ear,
tell me what I want to hear,
it's wrong, but I know I'm not the only one
to postpone cries,
letting lies
turn to lullabies

When I wake to face the day,
I shall find a better way
to accept the truth unkind,
my mind, like eyes when you draw the blind
to reveal the sun,
shall adjust,
but let last night's lies linger like dust,
before the morning brings its inevitable gust

Even when
I am happy
the voice inside my head
still likes to question
something

Fickle

I am the most complicated,
easy going
complication
you will ever meet,
the most organised mess,
the most emotionally reckless.
A rock,
that will shatter with a glare
or be the one to hold mountains together.
Now I know what Nick meant
when he said he is
within and without.
I am here and not here,
a human feeling utterly unhuman.
I will destroy myself,
heal myself,
love,
hate,
feel myself,
begging for love,
when sometimes I'm unsure
if there's any left
in this world

the finding a spark

I doubt the quality of the work I do every day,
but if I stop creating it,
that's where the real doubt starts

A Note on Creativity

Artists may paint
in strokes,
writers may write
in lines,
but creativity
is not linear.
It comes and goes
like the tide.
We cannot be angry
when the ocean
throws up seaweed
instead of pearls,
nature is not predictable
and neither are we,
creativity
ebbs
and flows,
sinks
and floats,
but it is not linear

nieve

No day is ever the same,
some days are bitter,
some days are sweet,
but it is the not knowing
that keeps me sane

Make a coffee,
have it black,
open a window,
stretch your back,
light a candle,
watch it burn,
take a pen,
write and
learn

    - This is how I learnt about myself

I have learnt that you cannot simply
write away your problems,
but it is a pretty good place
to start

Flood of Words

I choose to let words flow out of me like a river
because rivers are how you get to oceans,
and I let my emotions pour out
like unpredictable weather,
because sunshine and rain
is how you make rainbows.
We all have the ingredients within us
to make magic
on paper,
to stop wars
with words,
in
droplets,
we can create r i p p l e s

I used to care so much about
what others think,
but I came to realise
that opinions
are just that -
opinions,
and who's opinion
matters more
than your own?

It is ironic that our critics
are so often
our most loyal followers

Space

There is space here.
For you,
for me,
for all of us.
We do not have
to block each other out,
take turns
to grow.
It does not matter
how worthy
you think you are,
how big, how tall,
there is space here.
There is space
for us all

Bully

I was short
and you were tall,
now I've grown,
you haven't at all,
you were strong
and I was weak,
now my words echo
while you
can barely speak

You are like a kinder egg
without a prize

Thank you for teaching me
that the prettiest packaging
is not always the most appealing

on love and life

Why am I so keen to criticise myself?
I have not even lived half of my life yet,
of course I am still growing

Opinions

I have hairs on my face
that you might say
are not very womanly

I have strong opinions
about many things
of which you won't agree

My clothes reveal skin
that you don't find
appropriate to see

And all this might matter
if only I cared
what you thought of me

Why should a woman's body
be kept trimmed
like a garden,
when it was designed
to be a forest

The mirror
only reflects
the way you see yourself

Paint your face in the morning,
not because you need to,
but because it brings you great joy
to apply the finishing touches
to a masterpiece

Skin

This is the skin I am in,
this is how I came,
these marks are proof of where I've been
and how I still remain.
This is how I begin,
to love how I begun,
and the changes I have made,
and who I've now become.
I love these broken parts of me,
these parts they keep me sane,
they remind me I am human,
and that human is okay

You can choose
to make the body you live in
a house
or a home

nieve

There is no book on my shelf
that doesn't have a bent spine,
scribbled pages,
a folded corner.
They, like you
have been used
more than a few times.
But my darling,
just because you have been read,
does not mean you are damaged

San Francisco

San Francisco
baby
left me dry eyed,
slightly crazy,
broke,
you bound me up,
opened my heart
as if to choke
and I don't know
if I'll travel again,
down the windy
Lombard street,
but I'll remember
the dizzy feeling
of being
a young woman
in a big
San Franciscan
dream

- How cities change us

Barcelona

Barcelona, when I arrived,
I was an open door,
I didn't know what I know now,
how could I have known, *before*

Barcelona, when I hated you,
alone on the first floor,
I spied on strangers I didn't know
and knew I'd never care for

Barcelona, when I loved you,
I loved you to the core,
from every mosaic and rose-clad tile
to every wave upon the shore

Barcelona, when I left you,
I left only
wanting more

Laughter
music
smiling
dancing

Some things need no translation

This City

This city was not kind to me,
it did not want me here.
I was another tourist
who could not speak the language

But I was kind to this city,
I was kind to myself here,
I wandered round with fresh eyes
for hours and hours on end

I will not have left my mark,
I have no doubt that trains
continue to run,
birds continue to fly

But whenever I
look up at trees
or apartment buildings,
I will remember every detail

I will never stop looking,
observing,
with a curious eye,
a curious heart

Even at home,
the places you know so well,
there are always new paths,
new stories to tell

Thoughts From a Train

You may own a house
but that doesn't make it home,
home is not bricks,
home is not stone

You can never miss home,
you never leave it behind,
home is a feeling,
home is in your mind

Home, I've found,
has no name, no place,
I've felt at home
with just a suitcase

It's the people you're with,
the memories you share,
they're your ruby slippers,
so wear them everywhere

What Life is About

Life is not about
deadlines,
it is not about
waiting lines,
life is not about
fast cars,
it is not about
sleazy bars,
life is not about
paying rent,
it is not about
that fancy event,
gaining muscle,
hustle,
bustle,
or settling debt,
but now that I've told you
everything life is not about,
have you worked out
what it is yet?

on love and life

If you love what you do,
people will love what you do

- People love passion

Minutes

Just five more minutes,
I snooze my alarm,
thirty seconds
for the coffee machine to warm up.
It takes me twenty-five minutes to get to work,
that is how I've timed it.
I'm always that little bit early,
so I wait five minutes outside
for everyone else to arrive

My days are composed of insignificant minutes
like these.
They don't achieve much,
but to me they mean the most.
I have found
that it is not always about how much
you achieve
with your time,
but how you feel
in these little minutes that make up the day
when you are most alone

Spring Cleaning

One day
I ventured inside my mind.
They were so surprised
to find me there,
they had not prepared at all.
The room was a mess,
there was dust everywhere,
the windows had been blocked up
and the whole place looked
as if it hadn't seen light
for years.
No wonder I've been feeling so dark,
I say.
You're all fired,
I don't need you anymore,
from now on
I'm doing this on my own.
I took a broom
and started small.
It took time,
but soon it started
to look like a home again.
I threw away all the old files,
there is no reason
to hoard,
I hung curtains
around the windows,

nieve

from now on
I can choose
when to let the light in,
I aired the place out,
left peonies on the table,
and as I left
I turned around,
took one last look
and thought,
yes,
this is how it's meant to be,
now
I can breathe
again

on love and life

When we cry
we mimic the rain,
and that is so powerful

Growth

I've always admired flowers
for the way that they grow,
rooted and reaching
for the sun.
But we do not grow
like flowers.
Sometimes, growth
is three step forwards
and one step back.
Sometimes we run,
sometimes we crawl,
sometimes, it takes a storm
to make us move
at all.
But unlike flowers,
our growth
has no limit.
Reach for the sun
and you will get there

on love and life

Grief
just means that you have loved

Happy

When I was 6 years old
they asked me
who I wanted to be,
I said *something*

When I was 10 years old
they asked me
who I wanted to be,
I said *someone*

When I was 16 years old
they asked me
who I wanted to be,
I said *someone's*

Now when they ask me,
at 30, 40, 50
who I want to be

I say
it doesn't matter
as long as I'm happy

I just want to be happy

Opera

When I heard your quivering notes,
your voice and its obscurity,
I heard not just melody,
but soul.
Your voice that wavers
stabilised in my mind,
screaming of passion through words undefined,
and it sang, *you can do whatever you set your mind to*

nieve

We exist in every footprint
we ever leave

It's Okay

It's okay
to have days
where all you do
is cry

It's okay
to feel like
you might as well
not try

but what's not okay
is thinking
in any type of way

that these things
give you reason
not to stay

nieve

You are human.
Do not cry
because you have explored the depths
of what that means

The firefly
does not know
how long it has to live
yet it never fails
to light up
the night sky

Temporary

We are temporary.
I've known that from the start,
though I haven't always acted like it.
Life seems so fragile these days
but I don't know why I'm surprised.
Flowers
die,
re-grow,
stars
become black holes,
seasons change,
leaves fall,
the most beautiful things in this life
are temporary
after all

Home Comforts

Coffee machines and throw pillows,
vitamins and mirrored walls,
take it all away and ask yourself,
what do you have left,
do you still have a home?
If the answer is no, *go*

nieve

The key to life is much the same as love,
find a spark and
never let go

acknowledgements

To all the boys who played even the smallest role in my story - thank you for breaking my heart; teaching me how to heal.

To my family, who might not always understand me, but continue to support me in every possible way.

To Kate, my harshest critic, and therefore, my most trusted friend. Thank you for the countless hours you always give to me, for reading this book before it was a book, and for helping me believe that it could be a book.

To Lottie, for understanding, for listening and for always giving the best advice. You have helped me in ways you can't even imagine.

And of course, thank you to the rest of my glorious ladies, who taught me before anyone else what it means to love, and be loved.

This book is for you, it's about you, it is you. So thank you.

about the author

nieve is a 25-year-old poet and writer based in London. After receiving her bachelor of arts degree in English literature, she now continues her passion for all things writing by inspiring others as a secondary school English teacher.

Her debut poetry collection is a culmination of her experiences and her existence so far, centring around the two most universal themes of all: love, and life itself.

You can find her on Instagram and all other socials at @wordsbynieve

Or visit her website at www.wordsbynieve.com

If you enjoyed this book, please consider leaving a review; they are always appreciated.

www.ingramcontent.com/pod-product-compliance
Lightning Source LLC
Chambersburg PA
CBHW072049110526
44590CB00018B/3099